The Uncomplicated Art of Not Overthinking Retirement

Lee Busto

Published by Lee Busto, 2024.

THE UNCOMPLICATED ART OF NOT OVERTHINKING RETIREMENT

First edition. March 24, 2024.

ISBN: 979-8224551538

Written by Lee Busto.

For my two greatest loves,

To Oaklynn, who illuminates every day with her laughter and endless curiosity. May you always carry the magic of your toddler years into every adventure ahead.

And to Jennifer, my steadfast partner in all of life's chapters. Thank you for being the heart of our family and the grace that ties our stories together.

With all my love,

Lee

Disclosure

Investment advisory services offered through Foundations Investment Advisers, LLC, an SEC registered investment adviser. The content provided is intended for informational and educational purposes only. The views, statements and opinions expressed herein are those of the individual speaker(s) and not necessarily those of Foundations and its affiliates.

Any comments regarding safe and secure investments and guaranteed income streams refer only to fixed insurance products. They do not in any way refer to investment advisory products. Rates and guarantees provided by insurance products and annuities are subject to the financial strength of the issuing insurance company; not guaranteed by any bank or the FDIC. A Roth conversion may not be suitable for your situation. The primary goal in converting retirement assets into a Roth IRA is to reduce the future tax liability on the distributions you take in retirement, or on the distributions of your beneficiaries. The information provided is to help you determine whether or not a Roth IRA conversion may be appropriate for your particular circumstances. Please review your retirement savings, tax, and legacy planning strategies with your legal/tax advisor to be sure a Roth IRA conversion fits into your planning strategies.

This book discusses general concepts for retirement income planning and is not intended to provide investment, tax or legal advice. Any story in this book is fictional and intended to highlight a particular topic discussed in this book. No story should be treated to apply to the reader's individual circumstances. Individuals are urged to consult with their tax and legal professionals regarding these issues.

The Uncomplicated Art of Not Overthinking Retirement

Introduction

Retirement and investing – are two fundamental aspects of life that often leave us scratching our heads in confusion. We're inundated with advice to work hard, save diligently in a 401(k), and trust that someday, retirement will magically fall into place. But amidst these vague directives, crucial questions linger: How much money is truly "enough" for retirement? What investment strategies make sense for this significant chapter of life? And when should one begin collecting Social Security benefits? As an Investment Advisor Representative, I've encountered these pressing concerns repeatedly, each query echoing the universal anxiety surrounding retirement planning.

Let's confront the straightforward truth: planning for retirement could be more concise than it appears, yet it often languishes at the bottom of our priority list. This book aims to bridge that gap. While it won't miraculously transform you into a stock market savant overnight, it is a comprehensive guide to retirement planning, distilling complex concepts into digestible wisdom. Through practical advice and explanations, this book endeavors to render your retirement aspirations achievable and entirely within reach.

Guided by the timeless principle of KISS – "Keep It Simple Stupid," a fundamental principle ingrained in me from my days on the baseball field – I aim to infuse this book with clarity. My objective is crystal clear to ensure you grasp retirement and investing thoroughly, leaving no room for lingering uncertainties. Expect concise chapters that pack a punch without unnecessary jargon. In the spirit of injecting a dose of vitality into a typically mundane subject, a sprinkle of sarcasm will be liberally sprinkled throughout these pages. After all, who said retirement planning couldn't benefit from a touch of fun?

Get ready for an exciting and informative journey as we delve into the complicated world of retirement planning. I'll bring you along as we navigate this complex landscape with humor and intelligence. Join forces with me to revolutionize the typically mundane realm of retirement preparation, painting a dynamic canvas of endless possibilities.

Chapter 1
The Basic's

Let's delve deeper into the intricacies of retirement account basics, a foundational aspect of financial planning that often needs to be clarified. This realm has three primary types: pre-tax, after-tax, and Roth accounts. Each category offers distinct advantages and considerations, shaping one's financial future trajectory.

Firstly, let's navigate the terrain of pre-tax accounts, a realm well-known to many individuals seeking to bolster their retirement savings. This category encompasses 401(k)s, Traditional IRAs, 457s, 403bs, and Profit-Sharing Plans. The allure of pre-tax contributions lies in the immediate tax benefits they afford, echoing the age-old adage of "get your deduction today, pay lower taxes later." However, as we shall soon uncover, this seemingly advantageous proposition harbors its own set of caveats. While contributing to pre-tax accounts offers an upfront tax break, the inevitable reality is that nearly every dollar withdrawn during retirement is subject to taxation. Moreover, the taxation burden extends beyond one's lifetime, with beneficiaries inheriting pre-tax assets also bearing the brunt of taxation.

Conversely, though less common, the after-tax segment of retirement accounts merits attention for its distinctive features. Unlike their pre-tax counterparts, after-tax assets entail contributions that have already been taxed, sparing individuals from future taxation on the principal amount. However, any growth accrued within these accounts remains susceptible to taxation. Notably, a strategic maneuver involves rolling after-tax assets from a 401(k) to another account, with contributions directed towards a Roth account. At the same time, earnings are allocated to a pre-tax account, laying the groundwork for potential taxation.

Enter the Roth account – a beacon of innovation in retirement planning and a personal favorite for many astute investors. Whether in the form of a Roth IRA, Roth 401(k), Roth 457, or Roth 403b, these vehicles offer unparalleled advantages that set them apart from their counterparts. The hallmark feature of Roth accounts lies in their tax treatment: contributions are made with after-tax dollars, thereby exempting them from future taxation, including on any accrued growth.

This exceptional quality makes Roth accounts seem invincible, protecting contributions and earnings from taxes. Furthermore, tax-free distributions continue for beneficiaries, ensuring a smooth transfer of wealth without tax burdens.

Retirement planning can be pretty complex, especially regarding Social Security benefits. These benefits are vital for many retirees as they provide financial security. Understanding the nuances of Social Security benefits is essential, as your decisions can significantly impact your retirement journey. You can start receiving Social Security benefits as early as 62 or defer until age 70. However, each choice has distinct implications for benefit amounts and long-term financial stability. Navigating the intricacies of Social Security involves understanding a maze of rules and regulations. You must consider income thresholds and retirement age when determining eligibility for benefits and taxation.

As we journey through retirement planning, one constant emerges - taxes loom large, affecting our current and future finances. Despite being often neglected, it's crucial to consider the impact of taxes on retirement planning carefully. Strategic tax planning is critical to financial security. Every decision should aim to minimize taxes, ensuring that each dollar saved for retirement fulfills its purpose without being eaten away by excessive taxation.

In the following chapters, we shall embark on a comprehensive exploration of retirement planning, armed with knowledge, insight, and a keen eye for strategic decision-making. We shall unravel the complexities of retirement accounts, Social Security, and taxation through practical guidance and real-world examples, empowering readers to chart a course toward financial independence and security in their golden years. Join me on this journey as we navigate the twists and turns of retirement planning, illuminating the path toward a brighter, more prosperous future.

Chapter 2
The Objective

In retirement planning, the thread that binds every decision and strategy is clearly delineating our objectives. These objectives serve as the guiding star, illuminating the path toward a secure and fulfilling retirement. However, defining these objectives is not a one-size-fits-all endeavor; instead, it is a deeply personal and nuanced process that requires careful consideration of individual circumstances, aspirations, and values.

At the heart of this endeavor lies the pivotal question: What do we hope to achieve in retirement? For some, the goal may be to retire at a specific age, perhaps to coincide with Medicare eligibility or to pursue lifelong passions and interests. Others may aspire to achieve financial independence earlier, leveraging their savings and investments to escape the confines of traditional employment. Indeed, the concept of retirement itself has evolved in recent years, with individuals like football coaches Nick Saban and Bill Belichick demonstrating that age need not be a barrier to continued engagement and contribution in one's chosen field.

Once the retirement timeline is established, the next crucial step is determining the income level required to sustain the desired lifestyle. This involves meticulously examining current spending habits, encompassing everything from essential living expenses to discretionary indulgences such as travel and entertainment. It is necessary to approach this assessment with realism, acknowledging that life is unpredictable and unforeseen expenses may arise.

In addition to understanding the income needed to support our desired lifestyle, it is equally important to identify the sources of fixed income available during retirement. Social Security benefits, pension payments, and potential rental income shape our financial picture. However, the decision of when to claim Social Security benefits should not be taken lightly, as it can significantly impact long-term financial security. Opting to claim benefits earlier may provide immediate income but could result in reduced payments over the long term. Delaying benefits can lead to higher monthly payments but necessitates drawing on other sources of revenue in the interim.

Moreover, as we contemplate our retirement objectives, it is essential to consider the long-term growth potential of our assets. Setting realistic expectations for investment returns is crucial, as overly optimistic projections can lead to disappointment and financial strain down the road. While past market performance may offer insights into potential returns, tempering expectations and adopting a conservative approach to asset growth is essential.

Exploring the vast potential of Roth conversions and employing various tax-efficient strategies emerges as a crucial pursuit in this financial landscape. Roth accounts stand out with their advantages, such as facilitating tax-free withdrawals during retirement and enabling the seamless transfer of assets to beneficiaries without the burden of taxation. Through meticulous planning and strategic maneuvers, individuals can navigate the tax terrain adeptly by converting pre-tax assets into Roth accounts. This proactive approach mitigates tax liabilities and fortifies the longevity and stability of one's retirement income, ensuring a more secure financial future.

Ultimately, the process of defining retirement objectives is as much an art as it is a science. It involves reflecting on what we want, looking ahead, and being flexible. By taking the time to articulate our goals and aspirations, we empower ourselves to make informed decisions that will shape our financial future for years to come. So, whether you're dreaming of an early retirement filled with leisurely pursuits or envisioning a more gradual transition into your golden years, the key is clearly defining and pursuing your objectives with purpose and determination.

Chapter 3
Navigating the Investment Landscape

As we move closer to our retirement goals, we must focus on creating an investment strategy to guide us through the unpredictable market. However, we must be cautious and aware of the complexities of asset management and risk mitigation. We can no longer rely on simply choosing a few stocks to invest in. Success in today's volatile market requires a multifaceted approach that balances opportunity with caution. While I cannot predict the future, I can offer valuable knowledge and experience to help navigate the maze of investment options.

Before embarking on our journey, let's take a moment to ponder the path ahead. The road to retirement is riddled with challenges, with storms brewing and unseen obstacles lurking. However, within these perils lie opportunities to enhance wealth, safeguard your future, and attain the financial independence you've long envisioned.

So, how do we navigate this treacherous terrain? How do we chart a course that will lead us safely to our destination? The answer lies in our investment strategy—a carefully crafted plan that will serve as our North Star, guiding us through the darkest nights and the stormiest seas.

But what, exactly, does this strategy entail? Is it simply buying low and selling high, chasing the latest hot stock or trendy investment? Far from it. Our investment strategy is a comprehensive framework encompassing various assets and instruments, each carefully chosen to serve a specific purpose.

The strategy is built on four pillars: risk management, liquidity, market-based investments, and fixed assets. As the old saying goes, diversification is the only free lunch in investing, a principle ingrained in our approach. By distributing our investments across different asset classes and sectors, we mitigate the impact of individual risks and enhance our prospects for success.

But diversification alone is not enough. We must also be vigilant in managing risk, recognizing that every investment has potential loss. My strategy includes robust risk management protocols designed to identify and mitigate potential threats before they derail our plans.

Furthermore, this diversified approach seamlessly integrates with our distribution strategy, ensuring a steady and reliable income stream during retirement while preserving capital for the long term.

In the following pages, we'll explore these pillars in detail, examining the strategies and tactics to help us navigate the investment landscape confidently and clearly. So, dear reader, strap in and prepare for an adventure that will take us to the very heart of the financial world and beyond.

Chapter 4
Navigating The Tides of Risk

As the sun sets on your career and the retirement horizon draws near, a new journey begins—one fraught with uncertainties and challenges. Yet, amidst the shifting sands of economic fortune, one principle stands tall as a lighthouse guiding your financial ship: risk management.

In the tranquil waters of a bull market, it's easy to feel invincible, lulled into a false sense of security by the gentle waves of prosperity. But wise sailors know that storms can arise suddenly, casting their vessels into turbulent seas. Likewise, in finance, economic headwinds can buffet your retirement plans, threatening to capsize your dreams.

Thus, as you chart your course toward retirement, risk management must be the cornerstone of your strategy. This vital task involves more than just watching the stock ticker or monitoring interest rates—it's about safeguarding your hard-earned savings against the whims of the market.

At the heart of our approach lies a trio of guiding stars: liquidity, principal preservation, and long-term growth. Like the sturdy pillars of a fortress, these objectives form the bedrock upon which your financial security rests.

First and foremost is liquidity—the ability to access cash when needed most. Just as a sailor keeps his emergency supplies close at hand, so too must you ensure that your financial lifeboat is well-provisioned. Whether it's unexpected medical expenses or a sudden downturn in the market, having ready access to funds can mean the difference between weathering the storm and foundering on the rocks.

Equally important is preserving principle—safeguarding your nest egg against the erosive forces of inflation and market volatility. Like a skilled navigator, you must avoid treacherous waters and risky investments that could jeopardize your hard-earned gains. Instead, focus on conservative strategies prioritizing capital preservation, ensuring your financial ship remains steady in adversity.

Being cautious with your finances is essential, but you need to do more than save money for proper financial security. You need to invest in growth, just like a tree needs to spread its roots deep into the earth to survive a storm. By balancing risk and reward, you can use compound interest and watch your savings grow. This will help you reach your financial goals and enjoy a prosperous retirement.

Ultimately, the journey to retirement is not for the faint of heart. It requires courage, determination, and, above all, a keen eye for risk. But fear not, fellow traveler, for with a steady hand on the wheel and a clear vision of your goals, you can navigate the tides of uncertainty and chart a course to a brighter tomorrow.

Chapter 5
The Power of Cash Reserves

Cash is a crucial part of retirement planning. It is often ignored compared to stocks and bonds, but it provides financial flexibility and helps in uncertain times. Cash is a vital foundation of economic security and can be utilized to secure our financial future. So, what makes cash so important, and how can we use it?

In this chapter, we explore cash reserves and their significance in retirement planning and uncovering strategies for building and maintaining these essential resources.

Cash is central to our portfolio, providing stability in an ever-changing landscape. Unlike stocks and bonds, whose values fluctuate with the whims of the market, cash remains steadfast—a reliable source of liquidity in times of crisis.

But cash's value extends beyond mere financial security. It also offers peace of mind, allowing retirees to sleep soundly, knowing they have a cushion to fall back on in emergencies. Whether it's unexpected medical expenses, home repairs, or simply a desire to splurge on a dream vacation, cash provides the flexibility to handle life's curveballs easily.

While the importance of cash reserves is evident, the challenge lies in building and maintaining them over time. For many retirees, the ideal cash reserve is equivalent to at least one year's worth of living expenses—a buffer large enough to weather most storms without having to dip into long-term investments.

However, building a cash reserve is only half the battle. The real challenge lies in replenishing it over time, ensuring it remains sufficient to meet your needs as they evolve. This requires a strategic approach that balances the desire for growth with the need for liquidity.

One effective strategy for replenishing cash reserves is allocating a portion of your investment portfolio to highly liquid assets with relatively low risk. This might include money market funds, short-term bonds, or a high-yield savings account. Maintaining a diversified portfolio of cash equivalents ensures that your cash reserves remain robust and accessible, even during market turmoil.

Indeed, the adage holds true: cash is king, especially in retirement. It's not just about facilitating day-to-day transactions; it's about wielding financial power and security. Retirees who prioritize building and maintaining a substantial cash reserve gain a significant advantage. They can confidently navigate life's uncertainties, knowing they have the liquidity to handle any situation. So, embrace the reign of cash and let it be your ally on the journey to a prosperous retirement.

Chapter 6
Riding the Waves: Navigating Market-Based Investments

In the tumultuous seas of retirement planning, market-based investments stand as both the beacon of hope and the disruption of uncertainty. These assets, ranging from individual stocks to equity funds, promise long-term growth but also harbor the ever-present volatility risk.

In this chapter, we explore the heart of market-based investments, exploring their potential rewards and pitfalls and charting a course for navigating the market's ups and downs.

Market-based investments form the bedrock of our investment strategy, offering the potential for substantial returns over time. Whether it's investing in individual companies with promising growth prospects or diversifying through equity funds, these assets hold the key to building wealth and securing a comfortable retirement.

However, with great potential comes significant risk. The value of market-based investments is inherently tied to market conditions, meaning they can experience considerable fluctuations in value over short periods. Economic downturns, geopolitical tensions, and unforeseen events can all impact market performance, leaving investors vulnerable to losses and uncertainty.

Given the inherent volatility of market-based investments, our approach is one of strategic navigation rather than reckless abandon. We recognize that attempting to time the market or predict short-term movements is a fool's errand, destined to end in frustration and disappointment. Instead, we focus on building a diversified portfolio of market-based assets, carefully allocating resources to maximize returns while minimizing risk.

One key aspect of our strategy is leveraging market upswings to replenish cash reserves. By systematically rebalancing our portfolio during periods of growth, we ensure that we have ample liquidity to weather downturns without being forced to sell investments at a loss. This disciplined approach preserves capital and positions us to capitalize on future opportunities.

Risk management is paramount in the market's ever-changing landscape. While market-based investments offer growth potential, they also expose investors to the risk of significant losses. By adopting a disciplined approach to asset allocation, diversifying across different sectors and asset classes, and periodically rebalancing our portfolio, we aim to mitigate risk while maximizing returns over the long term.

Market-based investments are a double-edged sword, offering the potential for substantial rewards alongside significant risks. By adopting a disciplined and strategic approach to asset allocation, we aim to navigate the market's ups and downs confidently, leveraging opportunities for growth while safeguarding against volatility and downside risk. Therefore, heed the wisdom of the market and allow it to steer you toward a secure and prosperous retirement.

Chapter 7

Anchors of Stability: Navigating Fixed Assets for Growth and Stability

In the dynamic landscape of retirement planning, fixed assets are the bedrock of stability, providing a steady foundation to build your financial future. In this chapter, we explore the role of fixed assets in preserving principal while capturing growth opportunities. From traditional bond funds to alternative options like multi-year CD ladders and annuities, we delve into the diverse array of investment vehicles that offer stability and growth potential, ensuring that your retirement portfolio remains resilient in the face of market volatility.

Fixed assets are crucial to our investment strategy as they offer stability and predictability in a constantly fluctuating market environment. While traditional mutual funds or ETF bond funds have been popular for their liquidity, they can also expose investors to losses and interest rate risks. In response, we look for alternative options that balance stability and growth, allowing us to preserve principal while achieving returns.

One such alternative is the multi-year CD ladder, a strategy involving staggering investments in deposit certificates with varying maturity dates. This approach not only offers the security of FDIC insurance but also provides a steady stream of income as CDs mature, allowing for periodic replenishment of cash reserves without sacrificing growth potential.

A more sophisticated investment option is to purchase individual bonds or create a bond ladder consisting of individual bonds. While this approach restricts our ability to access funds until the bond reaches maturity, which typically ranges between 5 to 30 years, it offers a stable stream of coupon payments throughout the bond's lifespan. It's important to note that these options are only partially risk-free as they involve both default and interest rate risks.

Another option worth considering is annuities, which offer a guaranteed income stream over a specified period. While annuities may not be suitable for everyone, they can provide a reliable source of income in retirement, particularly for those seeking to supplement Social Security and other retirement benefits.

Additionally, fixed index annuities are an intriguing option for investors looking for downside protection and the ability to participate in market upside. These annuities offer a unique blend of stability and growth potential, allowing investors to shield their principal from market downturns while benefiting from favorable market performance.

Ultimately, the key to success lies in striking the right balance between stability and growth. By diversifying across asset classes and investment vehicles, we aim to mitigate risk while capturing growth opportunities.

Fixed assets serve as anchors of stability in the tumultuous seas of retirement planning, providing a reliable source of income and preserving principal in the face of market volatility. By exploring alternative options and striking the right balance between stability and growth, you can navigate the complexities of the financial markets with confidence and achieve your long-term financial goals. So, whether you're nearing retirement or just beginning your journey, remember that fixed assets are essential building blocks of a secure and prosperous retirement.

Chapter 8
Navigating Distribution Planning in Retirement

As you embark on your retirement journey, shifting your focus from accumulation to distribution is essential. While saving diligently for retirement is undoubtedly crucial, how you manage and withdraw your savings in retirement can significantly impact your financial security and longevity. In this chapter, we'll explore the importance of distribution planning, shed light on common pitfalls, and offer strategies to help you navigate this critical phase of your financial journey.

Distribution planning is the process of strategically withdrawing funds from your retirement accounts to meet your living expenses while minimizing taxes and preserving your savings for the long term. Unlike during your working years, when your primary goal may have been to accumulate wealth in retirement, your primary concern shifts to generating a reliable income stream that will sustain you throughout your golden years.

The stakes are high when it comes to distribution planning. A misstep or oversight could have costly consequences, potentially jeopardizing your financial security and lifestyle in retirement. Consider this: withdrawing too much from your retirement accounts too soon could deplete your savings prematurely, leaving you vulnerable to economic hardship later in life. On the other hand, withdrawing too little may result in missed opportunities to enjoy your retirement years to the fullest or leave behind a larger-than-intended estate tax burden for your heirs.

One of the most common pitfalls in distribution planning is failing to account for the impact of taxes. While it's tempting to focus solely on maximizing your after-tax income, overlooking the tax implications of your withdrawals could result in significant tax liabilities down the road. For example, withdrawals from traditional retirement accounts such as 401(k)s and traditional IRAs are generally subject to income tax, while withdrawals from Roth accounts may be tax-free. By strategically coordinating withdrawals from different account types, you can minimize your tax burden and maximize your after-tax income.

Another common mistake is underestimating your life expectancy and longevity risk. With advances in healthcare and lifestyle factors, many retirees live longer than ever. You must plan for a potentially lengthy retirement to avoid outliving your savings. By incorporating longevity risk into your distribution planning, you can ensure that your income will last as long as you need, providing peace of mind and financial security in your later years.

Furthermore, overlooking the impact of inflation on your retirement income can erode your purchasing power over time. In comparison, inflation may seem like a distant concern. Even relatively low inflation rates can significantly impact your standard of living throughout a long retirement. By incorporating inflation-adjusted income streams, such as Social Security or certain types of annuities, into your distribution plan, you can help protect yourself against the erosive effects of inflation and maintain your purchasing power throughout retirement.

So, how can you ensure a successful distribution plan that meets your needs and safeguards your financial future? Here are a few strategies to consider:

- **Develop a Comprehensive Plan:** Take a holistic approach to distribution planning by considering all sources of retirement income, including Social Security, pensions, annuities, rental properties, and investment accounts. By coordinating these income streams strategically, you can optimize your retirement income and minimize taxes.

- **Consider Your Withdrawal Sequence:** Determine the most tax-efficient order for withdrawing funds from your retirement accounts. For example, consider withdrawing from taxable accounts first, followed by tax-deferred accounts, and finally, tax-free accounts like Roth IRAs. This sequencing can help minimize your tax liability and preserve your savings for the long term.

- **Plan for Longevity:** Incorporate longevity risk into your distribution plan by ensuring that your income streams are sufficient to cover your retirement expenses. Consider purchasing annuities or other guaranteed income products that provide lifetime income to protect against the risk of outliving your savings.

- **Monitor and Adjust:** Regularly review and adjust your distribution plan as needed to accommodate changing circumstances, such as market fluctuations, changes in tax laws, or unexpected expenses. By staying proactive and flexible, you can adapt your plan to meet your evolving needs and goals throughout retirement.

If you still need to catch on, distribution planning is like the cherry on top of your retirement planning sundae. The crucial, often overlooked, but oh-so-delightful part can make or break your financial future. So, if you're feeling brave enough to tackle this maze of tax codes, investment strategies, and longevity risk, then by all means, dive right in.

But seriously, understanding distribution planning is like deciphering a cryptic puzzle designed by the IRS. Navigating the myriad of tax implications, withdrawal strategies, and market fluctuations requires a ninja's finesse and a saint's patience. And let's not forget the joy of trying to predict how long you'll live—because who doesn't love playing the world's most stressful guessing game?

Chapter 9
The Tax Maze

Before we delve into the intricacies of taxes, let's set the record straight: I'm not a CPA, and I'm not here to dispense tax advice. For personalized guidance on tax matters, it's crucial to consult with a certified professional—someone like your trusted CPA or, if you're inclined, consider partnering with a firm like mine, equipped with its own CPA expertise. What follows isn't counsel; it's a journey through the insights I've gathered from numerous CPAs and the myriad client scenarios I've navigated. So, without further ado, let's jump right in.

Taxes are often relegated to the sidelines when discussing retirement planning, overshadowed by weightier matters like when to start cashing in on Social Security or how to craft the perfect investment portfolio. But make no mistake, my friend, taxes are the silent puppeteer pulling the strings behind the scenes, exerting a profound influence on the fate of your retirement nest egg. Consider this scenario: a blissfully retired couple, aged 60, boasting a handsome $1,000,000 in their retirement coffers, with a staggering $750,000 nestled snugly in pre-tax accounts. It's smooth sailing. Wrong.

Fast forward to age 73, when the specter of Required Minimum Distributions (RMDs) comes knocking; even with a modest 5% average return on their investments, their combined balance swells to a princely $1,413,518.27. But here's the kicker: their first RMD at age 73 would be a hefty $53,367.43, and by age 83, they'd have drawn down a whopping $750,593.57 in RMDs, leaving them with a still-impressive balance of $1,474,626.79, thanks to those steady 5% returns.

But here's the rub: they've already paid taxes on that initial $750,000 when they were sprightly 60-year-olds, and yet, they'll still be on the hook for taxes on the remaining balance. So, who emerges as the real winner in this tax tango? Spoiler alert: it's not the retiree.

It's abundantly clear that the government stands to benefit handsomely from the continued growth of retirement accounts, as evidenced by the gradual uptick in the RMD age. Initially set at the ripe old age of 70 1/2, it's been nudged up to 73, and now, whisperings in the wind suggest it might inch its way toward 75. But why, you ask? Ah, therein lies the million-dollar question. Could it be a cunning ploy to snag a larger slice of the pie from surviving spouses, or perhaps a tricky maneuver to expedite tax collection on inherited balances?

Imagine if they had executed Roth conversions earlier in their retirement planning. They could have strategically managed their tax liabilities in retirement, potentially reducing the impact of RMDs. By converting funds to a Roth IRA, they could have shielded a portion of their retirement savings from future taxation, thereby preserving more of their hard-earned wealth for themselves and their heirs.

Chapter 10
Navigating the Tax Maze: Maximizing Your Opportunities

Few obstacles loom as ominously in the vast landscape of retirement planning as taxes. Yet, within the intricate web of tax regulations lies a realm of opportunity waiting to be unlocked. It's time to embark on a journey of tax enlightenment, where strategic planning and savvy decision-making pave the way to financial prosperity.

Imagine our protagonists, a couple in their late fifties, standing at the threshold of retirement with dreams in their hearts and a substantial nest egg in hand. Their financial landscape is ripe for transformation, with $600,000 in bank accounts and an additional $250,000 tucked away in traditional IRAs.

Meet the husband, aged 58, poised to bid farewell to the daily grind at 60, while his wife, an energetic 50-year-old, enjoys the freedom of early retirement. With an annual income of $120,000 and their mortgage long since paid off, they have a comfortable cushion to navigate the road ahead.

Now, let us unveil a strategic masterpiece crafted to maximize their financial opportunities – the art of tax optimization. Under the guidance of a seasoned CPA, we devise a plan to leverage the standard deduction for married couples, a valuable tool in the arsenal of tax planning.

By strategically utilizing this deduction from their IRA assets each year, whether by depositing funds into savings or executing a Roth Conversion, we create a pathway to tax-free withdrawals totaling an impressive $204,000 over seven years. But our tale does not end there, for a crucial decision awaits as our protagonist approaches age 66 – when to activate Social Security benefits.

We carefully consider delaying activation until age 67, ensuring that none of his Social Security benefits are subject to taxation. This strategic move maximizes their retirement income and minimizes their tax burden, allowing them to retain more of their hard-earned savings.

As our heroes emerge victorious from the clutches of taxation, their financial fortress stands fortified against the ravages of required minimum distributions (RMDs). In the event of the husband's passing, his widow is spared the burden of RMDs while also enjoying a higher Social Security benefit, thanks to their strategic decision-making.

Embrace this narrative of financial ingenuity. By embarking on a journey of tax optimization, you, too, can unlock the hidden potential within your retirement plan. Armed with knowledge and guided by expert advice, you can navigate the complexities of the tax code with confidence, emerging triumphant on the path to financial freedom.

Chapter 11

Leveraging Qualified Charitable Distributions (QCDs) for Tax-Efficient Giving

As retirees, many of my clients often find themselves contemplating not just their financial legacy but also their charitable impact. Fortunately, a powerful tool allows us to marry these two aspirations seamlessly: Qualified Charitable Distributions (QCDs). In this chapter, we'll explore QCDs, how they work, and the benefits they offer for tax-efficient giving in retirement.

Qualified Charitable Distributions, or QCDs, are a tax-savvy strategy for individuals RMD aged or older with traditional IRAs. With a QCD, you can transfer funds directly from your IRA to a qualified charity without incurring income tax on the distribution. This means the amount donated through a QCD is excluded from your taxable income, offering potential tax savings.

The process of making a QCD is relatively straightforward. Here's how it works:

- **Eligibility**: To be eligible to make a QCD, you must be at least 70½ years old at the time of the distribution. QCDs are only allowed from traditional IRAs, not employer-sponsored retirement plans like 401(k)s.

- **Distribution Limit**: The maximum amount you can donate through a QCD in a given year is $100,000 per individual.

This limit applies to the total amount of QCDs each individual makes, regardless of how many IRAs they own.

- **Direct Transfer**: The distribution must be directly from your IRA to the qualified charity. You cannot receive the funds yourself and then donate them to charity; they must go directly from the IRA custodian to the charitable organization.

- **Qualified Charities**: QCDs can only be made to qualified charitable organizations recognized by the IRS. This includes churches, nonprofit schools, hospitals, and public charities. Donor-advised funds and private foundations are not eligible recipients for QCDs.

Here are just a few of the benefits from doing a QCD:

- **Tax Savings**: The most significant benefit of QCDs is the potential for tax savings. Since the distribution is excluded from your taxable income, you can lower your adjusted gross income (AGI) and potentially reduce your tax liability.

- **Fulfill RMD Requirements**: QCDs can be used to satisfy your required minimum distributions (RMDs) for the year. This allows you to fulfill your RMD obligations while supporting charitable causes without adding to your taxable income.

- **Simplicity and Convenience**: Making a QCD is a straightforward process that requires minimal paperwork. By working directly with your IRA custodian and the charitable organization, you can streamline the donation process and ensure that your funds are put to good use.

- **Impactful Giving**: Donating directly from your IRA can impact the charitable causes you care about most. Whether it's supporting education, healthcare, or humanitarian efforts, QCDs offer a tax-efficient way to support organizations that align with your values.

While QCDs offer significant benefits for tax-efficient giving, there are some important considerations to keep in mind:

- **Consult with a Financial Advisor**: Before making a QCD, it's essential to consult with a qualified financial advisor who can assess your financial situation and determine if it aligns with your charitable goals.

- **Be Mindful of Contribution Limits**: QCDs offer tax advantages but are subject to annual contribution limits. To maximize the tax benefits of your donations, stay within the $100,000 limit per individual.

- **Keep Records**: It's essential to maintain accurate records of your QCDs for tax reporting purposes. Obtain a written acknowledgment from the charitable organization for each donation to substantiate your tax deductions.

- **Review Charitable Intentions Regularly**: As your financial situation and charitable priorities may change over time, reviewing your charitable intentions regularly and adjusting your giving strategy accordingly is essential.

Qualified Charitable Distributions (QCDs) offer a tax-efficient way for retirees to support charitable causes while minimizing their tax burden. By leveraging the benefits of QCDs, you can make a meaningful impact on the organizations you care about most while optimizing your retirement savings for tax efficiency. Consult a qualified financial advisor and tax professional to ensure QCDs align with your financial plan and charitable goals.

Chapter 12
Tax Tale Twists

Let's embark on a journey through the tangled maze of financial misconceptions and untangle one of the stickiest webs—the notion that grabbing all possible tax deductions now leads to lower taxes in retirement. It's a tempting idea, no doubt. After all, who wouldn't want to save a buck today and worry about taxes later when they're hopefully in a lower bracket?

Picture this: you're cruising through your prime at 35, tossing a cool $20,000 into your 401k and happily pocketing those tax breaks while lounging in a hefty 32% tax bracket. The plan? Retire someday in a lower bracket and revel in the savings. Sounds pretty straightforward. But let's hit the fast-forward button and zoom ahead to your golden years at 65.

That $20,000 you stashed away? It's not just sitting there gathering dust—it's blossomed into a juicy $121,162 thanks to solid growth. Not too shabby, huh? But here's where it gets interesting. When you finally decide to dip into that pot of gold, you might find yourself staring down the barrel of a much larger tax bill than you anticipated.

Let's say taxes have only dropped to 10% by then. If you'd paid taxes upfront and funneled your cash into a Roth 401k instead, you'd have coughed up just $6,400. But were you sticking with the traditional 401k route? Brace yourself for a hefty $12,000 tax bill. Ouch.

In the complex world of finance, the individuals who took advantage of tax deductions in the past may not always reap the greatest benefits. Sometimes, it's good old Uncle Sam, with his hand out and a grin, ready to collect his dues. Maneuvering through these fiscal complexities demands a vigilant approach and a well-crafted strategic blueprint.

Chapter 13

Navigating Medicare and Supplemental Plans

Welcome to the world of Medicare and supplemental plans, where understanding the ins and outs of healthcare in retirement can make all the difference. In this chapter, we'll take a practical approach to unraveling the complexities of Medicare while exploring the options for supplemental coverage that can enhance your healthcare experience during your golden years. There are more exciting things to discuss, but it's essential to understand, so I'm giving you the basics.

Understanding Medicare Essentials

- **Medicare Basics**: Let's start with the basics. Medicare is a federal health insurance program primarily for people aged 65 and older but also covers specific younger individuals with disabilities. Understanding the different parts of Medicare—Parts A, B, C, and D—is essential for making informed decisions about your healthcare coverage.

- **Eligibility and Enrollment**: Knowing when and how to enroll in Medicare is crucial. Most people become eligible for Medicare when they turn 65, but exceptions exist for those with disabilities or certain medical conditions. You must complete your initial enrollment period to avoid penalties, so staying informed about your eligibility and enrollment options is essential.

- **Coverage and Costs**: Medicare coverage includes hospital insurance (Part A), medical insurance (Part B), and prescription drug coverage (Part D). While many services are covered under Medicare, beneficiaries are still responsible for certain costs, such as premiums, deductibles, and copayments. Understanding these costs and how they fit into your budget is essential for planning your healthcare expenses in retirement.

Exploring Supplemental Coverage Options

- **Medigap Plans**: Medigap, also known as Medicare Supplement Insurance, is designed to fill the gaps in Medicare coverage, such as copayments, deductibles, and coinsurance. Private insurance companies offer these plans and can provide additional peace of mind by helping to cover expenses that Medicare alone does not.

- **Medicare Advantage Plans**: Medicare Advantage Plans, or Medicare Part C, are an alternative to traditional Medicare. Private insurance companies approved by Medicare offer these plans, often including additional benefits such as vision, dental, and hearing coverage. Medicare Advantage Plans may also offer prescription drug coverage, making them a comprehensive option for beneficiaries seeking additional benefits beyond original Medicare.

- **Prescription Drug Plans (Part D)**: Medicare Part D plans provide coverage for prescription drugs and are available to anyone enrolled in Medicare Part A or B. Private insurance companies offer these plans and vary in terms of covered medications, formularies, and costs. Choosing the right Part D plan can help ensure access to necessary medicines while minimizing out-of-pocket expenses.

Practical Tips for Medicare Enrollment and Management

- **Stay Informed**: Keep up-to-date with Medicare changes, deadlines, and coverage options to make informed decisions about your healthcare. Resources such as the Medicare website, educational materials, and trusted advisors can provide valuable information to guide your choices.

- **Review Your Coverage Annually**: Medicare plans and supplemental coverage options can change from year to year, so review your coverage annually during the open enrollment period is essential. Assess your healthcare needs, compare plan options, and make adjustments as necessary to ensure you have the coverage that best meets your needs.

- **Seek Assistance if Needed**: Navigating Medicare and supplemental coverage options can be complex, and it's okay to seek assistance if you have questions or need help understanding your options. Medicare counseling programs, insurance agents, and healthcare professionals can provide guidance and support to help you make informed decisions about your healthcare coverage.

Understanding Medicare and supplemental coverage options is essential for managing your retirement healthcare. By familiarizing yourself with the basics of Medicare, exploring supplemental coverage options, and staying informed about changes and deadlines, you can make confident decisions about your healthcare that support your overall health and well-being in retirement.

Chapter 14
Navigating Long-Term Care: Strategies for Financial Security

As we journey through the intricate landscape of retirement planning, long-term care is another aspect often overlooked until it's too late. Long-term care refers to services designed to help meet the medical and non-medical needs of individuals with chronic illnesses or disabilities who cannot care for themselves independently. With the cost of long-term care services soaring, developing strategies that provide financial security and peace of mind in the face of potential future care needs is crucial.

Traditional insurance policies have long been touted as the go-to solution for covering long-term care expenses. However, for many, including myself, these policies have significant drawbacks, such as rising premiums, limited coverage options, and the risk of paying for benefits that may never be used. As such, alternative strategies that leverage retirement assets and offer tax advantages have emerged as attractive alternatives.

- **Utilizing Retirement Assets for Long-Term Care:** One strategy gaining traction among retirees is using retirement assets, such as individual retirement accounts (IRAs) or 401(k) plans, to fund long-term care expenses. Individuals can tap into their nest egg by strategically withdrawing funds from these accounts to pay for qualified long-term care services while potentially enjoying tax benefits.

- **Long-Term Care Partnership Programs**: Several states offer Long-Term Care Partnership Programs, which allow individuals to protect a portion of their assets from Medicaid spend-down requirements by purchasing qualifying long-term care insurance policies. Under these programs, policyholders can access Medicaid benefits without depleting all their assets, providing a safety net for their financial security and heirs.

- **Hybrid Long-Term Care Insurance Policies:** These policies combine life insurance or annuities with long-term care coverage, allowing policyholders to access their benefits for either purpose. These policies provide a death benefit to beneficiaries if long-term care benefits are not utilized, addressing the concern of "use it or lose it" often associated with traditional long-term care insurance.

- **Using Health Savings Accounts (HSAs):** Health savings accounts (HSAs) offer another avenue for funding long-term care expenses. Contributions to HSAs are tax-deductible, and withdrawals for qualified medical expenses, including long-term care services, are tax-free. By contributing to an HSA while still in the workforce and allowing the funds to grow over time, individuals can build a dedicated pool of funds to cover future long-term care needs.

- **Tax Deductions for Long-Term Care Expenses**: It's worth exploring the tax deductions available for long-term care expenses. Qualified long-term care expenses, including nursing home care, assisted living facilities, and home health care, may be deductible under certain circumstances. By keeping detailed records of long-term care expenses and consulting with a tax professional, individuals can reduce their tax burden while financing their care needs.

THE UNCOMPLICATED ART OF NOT OVERTHINKING RETIREMENT

Long-term care planning is a critical component of comprehensive retirement planning. By exploring alternative strategies that leverage retirement assets, please take advantage of tax benefits, and offer flexibility in funding long-term care expenses, individuals can safeguard their financial security and meet their needs as they age. Consulting with a qualified financial advisor and tax professional is essential to developing a personalized long-term care plan that aligns with your goals and circumstances.

Chapter 15

Safeguarding Your Legacy: The Vital Role of Estate Planning

As we continue to navigate the intricate landscape of retirement planning, a crucial aspect often gets overlooked amidst the hustle and bustle of financial considerations: estate planning. While it may not be the most glamorous topic, it holds immense significance in ensuring that your legacy is preserved and your loved ones are provided for according to your wishes. In this chapter, we'll explore the importance of estate planning, delve into the benefits of various estate planning tools such as trusts, wills, and powers of attorney, and illustrate the consequences of neglecting this vital aspect of financial preparedness.

Estate planning is more than just drafting a will or designing beneficiaries for your retirement accounts. It encompasses a comprehensive strategy for managing and distributing your assets, minimizing taxes, and ensuring that your wishes are fulfilled in the event of your incapacitation or passing. By taking proactive steps to plan your estate, you can protect your loved ones from unnecessary legal battles, minimize tax liabilities, and leave a lasting legacy that reflects your values and priorities.

Disclaimer: I'm no estate planning attorney, so naturally, none of this is legal advice; it's just a light-hearted romp through the world of estate planning and tax-saving strategies.

Let's begin by exploring some of the critical components of estate planning:

- **Wills**: A will is a legal document that outlines your wishes regarding the distribution of your assets after your death. It allows you to designate beneficiaries for your property, appoint guardians for minor children, and specify any other instructions you wish to be carried out upon your passing. Having a will ensures that your assets are distributed according to your wishes and can help avoid disputes among family members.

- **Trusts**: Trusts are legal arrangements that allow you to transfer assets to a trustee, who holds and manages them on behalf of your beneficiaries. There are various types of trusts, each with its benefits. For example, a revocable living trust allows you to retain control of your assets during your lifetime while providing for their distribution to your beneficiaries upon your death. Trusts can also offer privacy, flexibility, and protection from creditors and probate courts.

- **Powers of Attorney (POA)**: A power of attorney is a legal document granting someone else the authority to decide if you become incapacitated. There are different types of POAs, including financial POAs, which authorize someone to manage your financial affairs, and healthcare POAs, which allow someone to make medical decisions on your behalf. Having a POA in place ensures that your affairs are handled by someone you trust and can help avoid the need for court-appointed guardianship.

Now, let's turn our attention to a cautionary tale illustrating the perils of neglecting estate planning. Meet the Smith family – a seemingly ordinary couple with two children and a modest estate comprising a family home, retirement accounts, and some investments. Like many families, the Smiths put off estate planning, assuming they had plenty of time to address it.

Tragically, fate had other plans. One day, Mr. Smith unexpectedly passed away due to a sudden illness, leaving behind a grieving widow and two bewildered children. In the absence of a will or estate plan, chaos ensued. The family home, retirement accounts, and investments were thrown into legal limbo, subject to lengthy court proceedings and bitter disputes among family members.

To make matters worse, without explicit instructions from Mr. Smith, his family was left in the dark about his wishes regarding end-of-life care and asset distribution. As a result, tensions ran high, relationships strained, and the family's grief was compounded by the stress and uncertainty of navigating the complex legal and financial intricacies of probate court.

Ultimately, the Smith family learned a harsh lesson about the importance of estate planning – a lesson that came at a steep cost in terms of time, money, and emotional turmoil. Their story is a stark reminder that estate planning is not just about protecting your assets; it's about safeguarding your loved ones' well-being and preserving harmony within your family long after you're gone.

Let the tale of the Smith family serve as a cautionary beacon, guiding you on your estate planning journey. Don't wait until it's too late—take proactive steps to plan your estate today, utilizing tools such as wills, trusts, and powers of attorney, and ensure that your legacy is protected and that your loved ones are provided for according to your wishes.

Chapter 16:
Maximizing Tax Efficiency with Irrevocable Trusts

Few tools offer the tax-saving potential and asset protection of irrevocable trusts in retirement planning. As retirees navigate the complexities of estate planning, understanding the nuances between revocable and irrevocable trusts is paramount to crafting a comprehensive strategy that optimizes tax efficiency and safeguards wealth for future generations.

I feel silly putting this again, but once again, as a friendly reminder, I am no estate planning attorney, so naturally, none of this is legal advice.

I do, however, want to make sure we understand the differences between a revocable and an irrevocable trust:

- **Revocable Trusts**: Also known as living trusts, revocable trusts are flexible estate planning tools that allow grantors to retain control over trust assets during their lifetime. With a revocable trust, the grantor can modify or revoke it anytime, making it a versatile option for individuals who wish to maintain flexibility and control over their assets. However, revocable trusts do not offer the same asset protection or tax benefits as irrevocable trusts, as trust assets are still considered part of the grantor's taxable estate.

- **Irrevocable Trusts**: In contrast, irrevocable trusts are permanent arrangements in which assets are transferred into the trust's ownership, with terms that cannot be altered or revoked by the grantor. Once assets are placed into an irrevocable trust, they are no longer considered part of the grantor's estate, offering protection from creditors, potential estate taxes, and probate proceedings. While irrevocable trusts may require relinquishing some control over trust assets, they provide enhanced tax benefits and asset protection compared to revocable trusts.

Tax-Saving Benefits of Irrevocable Trusts

- **Estate Tax Reduction**: Irrevocable trusts offer a powerful means of reducing estate taxes by removing assets from the grantor's taxable estate. By transferring assets into the trust, retirees can effectively minimize estate tax liability and ensure more of their wealth is preserved for future generations.

- **Gift Tax Exclusion**: Irrevocable trusts facilitate tax-efficient wealth transfer through gift tax exemptions. When assets are transferred into the trust, they may be considered gifts to the beneficiaries. By leveraging the annual gift tax exclusion and lifetime gift tax exemption, retirees can transfer assets to beneficiaries without incurring gift tax liabilities.

- **Income Tax Savings**: Depending on the trust structure, income generated by trust assets may be subject to lower tax rates than individual income tax rates. Certain irrevocable trusts, such as grantor trusts, allow the grantor to retain control over trust assets while still enjoying income tax benefits.

Implementing an Irrevocable Trust Strategy

- **Consult with a Trust Attorney**: Retirees should consult with a qualified trust attorney to assess their estate planning goals and determine the most appropriate type of trust for their needs. An experienced attorney can help draft legal documents and ensure the trust is structured to maximize tax efficiency and asset protection.

- **Transfer Assets to the Trust**: Retirees can transfer assets into it once the trust is established, effectively removing them from their taxable estate. These may include cash, investments, real estate, or other valuable assets.

- **Designate Trust Beneficiaries**: Careful consideration should be given to designating beneficiaries who will ultimately receive the trust assets. Retirees may also include asset distribution and management provisions to ensure the trust aligns with their estate planning goals.

- **Please review and Update Trust as Needed**: Estate planning is an ongoing process, and retirees should periodically review and update their irrevocable trust to reflect changes in their financial circumstances, tax laws, and family dynamics.

Consider the case of a retiree with a sizable estate valued at $10 million. By establishing an irrevocable trust and transferring assets into the trust, the retiree effectively removes those assets from their taxable estate, reducing potential estate tax liability. Additionally, income generated by the trust assets may be subject to lower tax rates, further enhancing tax efficiency and preserving wealth for future generations.

Irrevocable trusts represent a strategic tool for retirees seeking to minimize tax liabilities, protect assets, and ensure a legacy for their loved ones. By understanding the critical differences between revocable and irrevocable trusts and working with experienced professionals, retirees can harness the tax-saving potential of irrevocable trusts to achieve their estate planning goals with confidence and peace of mind.

Chapter 17
Putting It All Together

Alright, let's cut to the chase. Time is money. Here's your no-nonsense action plan for retirement without the unnecessary fluff.

- **Assess Your Current Financial Situation**: Take stock of your assets, liabilities, and income streams. This includes evaluating your retirement accounts, savings, investments, and outstanding debts. Understanding where you stand financially is crucial for charting your path forward.

- **Define Your Retirement Goals**: What does retirement look like for you? Consider factors such as desired lifestyle, retirement age, healthcare expenses, travel plans, and legacy goals. By clearly defining your retirement vision, you can tailor your financial plan to align with your aspirations.

- **Maximize Tax Efficiency:** Take proactive steps to minimize your tax burden now and in retirement. Consider strategies such as Roth conversions, which involve moving funds from traditional retirement accounts to Roth accounts to enjoy tax-free withdrawals in retirement. Consult with a tax professional to ensure you capitalize on all available tax-saving opportunities.

- **Optimize Social Security Benefits:** Evaluate the timing for claiming Social Security benefits based on your circumstances. Delaying benefits can result in higher monthly payments, providing a valuable source of guaranteed income in retirement. Explore claiming strategies such as file and suspending or restricting applications to maximize benefits for you and your spouse.

- **Diversify Your Investment Portfolio:** Review your investment portfolio to ensure it's appropriately diversified across asset classes, industries, and geographical regions. Consider your investment decisions, risk tolerance, time horizon, and retirement goals. Aim for a balanced portfolio that offers growth potential while mitigating risk.

- **Establish an Emergency Fund:** Build a robust emergency fund to cover unexpected expenses and weather financial downturns. Aim to set aside three to six months' worth of living expenses in a readily accessible account, such as a high-yield savings account or money market fund.

- **Create a Retirement Budget:** Develop a comprehensive budget that outlines your anticipated retirement expenses and income sources—factor in essential costs such as housing, healthcare, transportation, and discretionary spending. Use tools like retirement calculators to estimate your retirement income needs and adjust your budget accordingly.

- **Create a distribution strategy:** Identify your income sources each year. Plan for down and up markets while ensuring it aligns with your long-term tax strategy.

- **Stay Informed and Adapt:** Stay abreast of changes in tax laws, investment trends, and retirement planning strategies.

THE UNCOMPLICATED ART OF NOT OVERTHINKING RETIREMENT

Periodically review and adjust your financial plan as needed to reflect changes in your life circumstances, goals, and market conditions. Consider partnering with a trusted financial advisor to guide and support your retirement journey.

In addition to these fundamental steps, it's essential to consider specific strategies for estate and long-term care planning:

- **Establishing Trusts**: Trusts are powerful estate planning tools that allow you to control the distribution of your assets, minimize estate taxes, and provide for your loved ones according to your wishes. Consider establishing trusts such as revocable living trusts, irrevocable trusts, or special needs trusts to achieve your estate planning goals.

- **Drafting Wills and Powers of Attorney (POA)**: Wills are legal documents that outline your wishes regarding the distribution of your assets after your death. Powers of attorney authorize someone to make financial or healthcare decisions on your behalf if you become incapacitated. Work with an estate planning attorney to draft these essential documents and ensure they accurately reflect your intentions.

- **Long-Term Care Planning**: Long-term care planning involves preparing for the possibility that you may need assistance with activities of daily living as you age. Explore options such as long-term care insurance, Medicaid planning, and asset protection strategies to cover long-term care costs while preserving your assets for your heirs.

As we conclude our journey through this book, I sincerely hope you're departing with a wealth of knowledge and insights to empower your retirement planning endeavors. As a parting reminder, let's embrace the timeless principle of KISS - Keep It Simple, Stupid. Let's forge ahead confidently towards retirement with clarity and purpose as our guiding lights.

Retirement isn't a distant dream; it's a tangible reality within our reach. As we close this chapter and turn the final page, let's recognize that the power to shape our future lies not in complexity but in the simplicity of well-informed decision-making. With newfound wisdom, let's step boldly into the next chapter of our lives, poised to embrace retirement's opportunities and challenges. The journey continues, and the possibilities are endless.

If you ever need guidance or a chat, remember, I'm just a Google search away.

About the Author

Lee Busto is a seasoned investment advisor devoted to simplifying complex financial concepts and empowering individuals to achieve retirement goals. With over six years of experience in the financial services industry, Lee has honed his expertise in wealth management, retirement planning, and tax optimization strategies.

Beginning his professional journey in 2017 with Edward Jones, Lee quickly established himself as a dedicated advisor committed to providing personalized financial guidance. His unwavering commitment to excellence and client satisfaction earned him recognition within the industry.

Currently serving as an Investment Advisor at Alpha 1 Tax & Wealth, Lee continues to leverage his knowledge and expertise to assist clients in navigating retirement planning and investment management intricacies. As a Certified Retirement Planning Counselor (CRPC.) and an Accredited Asset Management Specialist (AAMS.), he brings specialized knowledge and tailored solutions to meet each client's unique financial needs.

Beyond his professional achievements, Lee boasts a diverse background encompassing athletics and academic accomplishments. A former college baseball player and a notable figure in the American Association, he understands the value of discipline, teamwork, and perseverance—traits he incorporates into his advisory role.

Lee holds a degree in Business Management with a minor in Finance from Montana State University Billings, where he developed analytical skills and deep financial understanding. His academic foundation and real-world experience position him as a trusted advisor capable of guiding clients through complex financial decisions.

Outside of work, Lee finds joy in family time. Happily married to Jennifer Busto, they reside in Centennial, Colorado, with their daughter and two cherished dogs. Lee's commitment to family and community reflects his integrity, compassion, and stewardship values—qualities evident inside and outside the office.

As an Investment Advisor, Lee Busto remains dedicated to helping individuals and families secure financial futures and achieve retirement dreams. With expertise, a personalized approach, and an unwavering commitment to client success, Lee continues positively impacting those he serves.